JOHN GREENING

# *To the War Poets*

Oxford*Poets*

**CARCANET**

First published in Great Britain in 2013 by
Carcanet Press Limited
Alliance House
Cross Street
Manchester M2 7AQ

www.carcanet.co.uk

A CIP catalogue record for this book is available from the British Library

ISBN 978 1 90618 808 5

The publisher acknowledges financial assistance from Arts Council England

Supported by
ARTS COUNCIL
ENGLAND

Typeset by XL Publishing Services, Exmouth
Printed and bound in England by SRP Ltd, Exeter

*To Jürgen Sandmann*

# *Acknowledgements*

Thanks are due to the editors of the following publications, in which poems in this book have appeared: *Agenda* ('Dropping Slow', 'Eglwys Llangwyfan', 'Hiraeth'); *Areté* ('To Rudyard Kipling'); *Bow-Wow Shop* ('Africa', 'The Island', 'In Trafalgar Square', 'So it Runs', 'Wadi Halfa'); Brindin Press website (translations of German poets); *Critical Quarterly* ('Aldermaston', 'Odyssey'); *Horizon Review* ('Cycle with Cytologist', 'Hounslow', 'The Train'); *Ink, Sweat & Tears* ('Forge House'); *The Interpreter's House* ('Waldo Williams in Perry'); *London Magazine* ('Causeway'); *Modern Poetry in Translation* (poems by Ernst Stadler, 'To the Sun (after Akhenaten)'); *Poetry Review* ('To Edward Thomas', 'Field', 'American Music'); *Quadrant* ('Colonial', 'Elgar', 'The Hope Valley Line'); *The Rialto* ('Reading John Clare'); *Seam* ('Middlesex', 'Piano'); *The Spectator* ('To John McCrae'); *Stand* ('To Laurence Binyon', 'To Julian Grenfell'); *The Times Literary Supplement* ('To Isaac Rosenberg', '11', 'Kentish'); *The Use of English* ('Yeats Dances', 'To Rupert Brooke').

'New World' featured in the programme for the Czech Philharmonic's concert at Symphony Hall, Birmingham and on the hall's website, for which I am grateful to Julie Boden. The Edmund Blunden verse letter appeared in the Blunden Online journal: thanks to Margi Blunden. 'Reading John Clare' was a contribution to the Festschrift for John Lucas, *Speaking English*. 'The Hope Valley Line' was included in *The Quadrant Book of Poetry* (ed. Les Murray). 'Awre' was used to preface Michael Greening's book *A Family Story*. I am grateful to Martin Carver for letting me take as an epigraph to 'The Mounds at Sutton Hoo' a quotation from his invaluable book *Sutton Hoo, Burial Ground of Kings?*

I owe a particular debt to my colleague Bill Skinner for organising the battlefields trip during which many of the verse letters were drafted. 'To One Who Was With Me' is dedicated to Helen Morrell, who was at the St Julien memorial with us when she received news of the death of her friend Dermot Sheridan in a helicopter crash.

# Contents

*Shall they return to beatings of great bells*
*In wild train-loads?*

Wilfred Owen

# *War*

## Georg Heym (1887–1912)

He's risen now, who slept so long,
He's risen from deep vaults, among
The day's remains. Huge and unknown
He stands. His black hands crush the moon.

Into the cities' evening crack
A shadow-frost falls, alien dark.
It makes the downtown bustle freeze.
Go quiet. Glance round. No one sees.

In side-streets, something grasps an arm.
A question. Answerless. Stay calm.
Far off, the bells are trembling thin
And stubble stirs on each sharp chin.

He's started. There, up on the fells
He's dancing, shouting: *Men! To kill!*
And when he shakes his dark head, chains
Of skulls go rattling round his brain.

A moving tower, he tramples out
The last of light. The river clots
As countless bodies staunch and dam
Its reedy flow. The white birds swarm.

He steeplechases through the night
This red wild-shrieking hound, and out
Of darkness spring night's secret shows,
Footlit as if by lava flows.

The fields are scattered with the pointed
Caps of a thousand flames; the hunted
Refugees below are thrust
Into the forest fires to roast.

From tree to tree, like yellow bats
The flames spread as inferno eats
Each forest. Rattling at the bars,
The stoker prods it till it roars.

A city sank into the reeking
Yellow, hurled itself, unspeaking.
But he stands vast above the glow
And shakes his torch three times to show

The storm-zagged clouds, the frigid wastes
Of darkness, he has seared this place
To ash; then brings to his dry lips
His brimstone spit: apocalypse.

## On the Eastern Front

### Georg Trakl (1887–1914)

The winter storm's mad organ playing
is like the *Volk*'s dark fury,
the black–red tidal wave of onslaught,
defoliated stars.

Her features smashed, her arms silver,
night calls to the dying men,
beneath shadows of November's ash,
ghost casualties heave.

A spiky no–man's–land encloses the town.
The moon hunts petrified women
from their blood–spattered doorsteps.
Grey wolves have forced the gates.

## Pleasure in Form

### Ernst Stadler (1883–1914)

First, bolts had to be broken, moulds
Be cracked before I let the world
Come bursting through new pipes: with form
Comes happiness and peace and warm
Contentment, yet I always need
To unplough what's been laid to seed.
Form wants to stifle and confine,
But I must sail beyond the line.
Form is pitiless, hard and clear,
Yet drives me to a stagnant mere.
Without the lifeline's dull insistence,
Life can sweep me out any distance.

## *In Despair*

August Stramm (1874–1915)


Overhead a stone's harsh warble
Night grinds glass
Times don't change
Stone
me.
Your
distant
glaze!

## *To August Stramm, Georg Trakl, Ernst Stadler, Georg Heym*

*In der Dämmrung steht er, gross und unbekannt*

No chair in this no-frills hostel –
designed for parties of schoolchildren
studying the war. Four pallets
on two bunk-beds, metal,
functional. Bed-bugs? Perhaps.

I had wondered, as we swiped
our plastic on the steel door
to get to sleep, what's underneath?
Now I have some idea, for this
is the German cemetery. A wreath,

massive, bronze, discoloured,
like a sea monster scalily
curled in on itself. Graves are
dark slabs, the memorials
monolithic; there is concrete.

Over forty thousand in this
square of earth, taped
as if for a crime-scene. Names
wait in strict formation, stand
to attention: *have we reached*

*yet nineteen thirty-three?*
Against the budding trees
and gathering clouds
are silhouetted four
huge, dumbstruck shapes.

# The Train

A name that pulls away effortfully
into a blue tunnel: that screen of blue
they use to graft the fantastic
on to the everyday in Hollywood
but here untouched

*nonscriptus*

puffing a life
towards its woodland terminus
where Horsted Keynes will come to mean
more than the terrifying hiss of steam
as parents insist you must go with them for the bluebells.

*

I turn the page and it is
*La Flèche d'Or*:

this golden arrow
straight to the heart

of France entrances me,
a sleeper across

the night seas
of these short

interminable years
before I turn the page

and there are words
and flesh to adore.

*

Was it Burton Bradstock we were returning from,
a long haul through flooded Dorset,
delay after delay,

when the train at last had ground to a halt
somewhere outside Castle Cary
and through a glass

smoking with gloom and shadowy work,
one cry – *we ain't got no steam!* –
made us hoot?

*

As if it weren't exciting
enough to be in a
camping coach
at Lyndhurst Station,

the steam trains hurtling
past us all night
through the New Forest,
through our dreams

of lines that switch
into a clearing
where King William
is assassinated –

*Oh, to be in England…*
was the April
headline as we woke
to a whiteout,

all the greenwood
blank as the pages
of a 1960s
domesday book.

*

Past Cologne,
past the Lorelei
and the Mouse Tower

we advance along
my green and narrow
sixteenth year

towards a dark
platform where the Sandmann
family reach out

and shake my hand
and take me in the car
blinking  blinking

over level crossings
that have forgotten
what once wept through

and blindly salute.

*Dover*

## *To Isaac Rosenberg*

The white cliffs are like all the paper they could not have –
the men who were not rich enough to be officers –
and that steady grey horizon is a never-ending pencil lead.

The channel is shifting with misty shapes of things that were said
but never written, for lack of paper, for want of pencils,
and beneath it currents and sands of what they really meant.

# The Island
## A to Z

*for Alan, Judy and Zaphod*

### A

The cliff edge fails,
exposing the bare white
narrative of a life
that has lost immunity.
The sun wheels round
to point at St Catherine.

You can play *Tambourine Man*
with light untroubled fingers
though you stumble over
the undercliff, its dormant
candlepower, Marconi's
whistle, a distress call.

There is cello music
in clouds, on the waves,
beating towards a refinery
that outgrows ancient forest,
playing a line of slow
inevitable open notes.

### TO

To live on the island is to accept the insignificance
of the mainland; it is to face up to the circular nature
of every bridleway, every road. It is to ally oneself

with those who stay, not those who visit for a day
and take the ferry back. It is to know where to go
searching for a peregrine high in columbaria of limestone

and confidently to follow the cinnabar moth down the ragwort
trail of extinct railway to pose with red squirrels
and a nut to crack. It is to speak with authority on Vectis

and the inland port of Alverstone, lost with all hands.


## Z

He watches the ferry leave.
He has a reputation

for failing obedience classes.
They expelled him from the kennels.

Once, he cocked his leg
in an attempt to dowse the fires.

Now he watches the ferry leave
without a sound.

But he can scent
in its wake a sleeping

sickness that drifts
through oil and bilge and weed

and is on the trail
of a place only good

for kindling, which people long
to escape, yet burn

to go home to:
somewhere dog-forsaken.

*To Wilfrid Gibson*

Though you didn't come to the trenches,
you wrote like a man who had been out

and were mighty popular for it. Best-seller.
Now, there in the mud of obscurity,

with your poor sight and your poor health and your
handsome inheritance from Rupert Brooke,

not to mention your reference from Robert Frost
as the worst snob he ever met in England,

sinking from decade to decade, you reach
for my help. But what can one keeper do?

It's twilight. The memory cards are not full
but they will be soon – look how they flash

and flash, like that lost beam from Flannan Isle.

# The Hope Valley Line

When our electrician was killed and the elms made a guard
of honour, saluting him, shoulders braided with green,
crowns embroidered – elm hateth man and waiteth –

it was just another in the long line of deaths in these
last months: the one who skidded down the dawn's
black ice and shivered into a fireball, the one

who lost control and died on a bridleway, and those
who did not perish but are paralysed from their youth down.
They have grown up around us, these tragedies. We glance

from what we are doing, moved, and feel relief
that death has not touched us directly yet,
but aware it is out there like some monstrous power

station in a field one passes in the train, the rain
weeping against the window but unable to trouble us.
The names of the places are announced, a roll call, flashed

on the visual display, but they mean no more than Hope meant
as I stopped there on the way to see my father's body
powerless, waiting for the arrival of the plywood coffin.

## 11

The young go down
along with the old
pushing November
from the front of their mouths

a childish rhyme
that makes an armistice
a cenotaph and marching
two by two,

fireworks all ground
to mash, and only
St Cecilia
to come, soothing

the day of Kennedy's
assassination from
her grassy knoll.
They keep on falling

revealing their black
buds that burn on
through the month
of the unknown soldier.

## 'Essex Farm', Yser Canal
### To John McCrae

We stop at Flanders Fields
and Owen's Coaches
draw up in the same layby.
Watery sun. A farmhouse
opposite has gone nowhere
since pneumonia blew you
away from this hole in
the canal side and it was
nineteen-eighteen. A factory
smoking silently through bare
pollarded poplars on the
far bank. Here, your poem.
There, parked tankers. The coach
driver is pacing, tie over
beer belly. No larks,
just the passing of traffic.
And no chance of a poppy
that isn't paper or plastic.
The children among the graves
are dressed as if they were
themselves a floral tribute.

## *To Robert Nichols*

I wonder which of my great-
grandparents or grandparents
kept this cutting from *The Times*
December 15th 1916?

It's yellow, of course, and
foxed across the words
'glorious' and 'sacrifice',
but complete. It's called

'The Battery', by you, and
'sketched in France, written
in England' after your three-
week spell in the line.

Less famous for fighting
Germans than hurling
a mangel-wurzel at
Lloyd George, for which

you were sent down,
though you were the 'King
of Oxford poetry'
with a blue pencil still

and knew how to throw
squibs, too: 'Peace is here.
Where is Alfred Noyes?'
You died in the war

in nineteen forty-four.

# Feast Day, Melchbourne

A yellow field for the cars to crawl into.
*Moonlight Serenade* from the Ouse Valley Band.
Tombola, bric-a-brac, a raffle, Pimm's
and nine-pins, coconut shies and strawberries.

We seem to have drifted back to the last war
when Glenn Miller gave his final performance
on this lawn in front of the manor house.
And even as we scramble behind the tractor

for a ride out of the grounds, the sounds of
*Perfidia* and *American Patrol*
accompany us into the oil-seed rape.
The farmer's boy, who's clinging to his trailer,

points through the bones of wych elm and thorn
and escalating nightshade to a chain-link fence
that flickers 'Danger Area' as we pass.
That's Coppice Wood, where they stored the mustard gas

for bombs. They tried to clear it in the fifties.
Thirty people a week were carted off
with burns. Abortions in cattle and sheep.
The air was black. His tractor turns to face

the slope where once the Knights Hospitaller
had their preceptory, before it was flattened
for baseball. When locals complained they were told
no way, there isn't nothing in the woods.

## *To Edmund Blunden*

Dear Blunden, here's a pastoral you'll appreciate,
uncensored too, though I am running out of pencil
and don't know what the Flemish is for sharpener.
It's Brueghelesque. The Yser Canal. One angler
with two rods and an (unnecessary) mud-brown brolly.
A bell is tolling midday-and-beyond behind me
and birdsong all around. One magpie. Two carrion crows.
A far cry from the throng back in the Flanders Fields Museum.
The tin helmet over the litter bin swings in the breeze
beside my metal bench. There are cyclists. And a lady's
terrier snaps and growls at someone's knapsack. It is all
unimaginable. The great deceit of Spring. Shout, *April
Fool, Ypres is rubble, the dead unburied, the war's
going on still...* I cough and cough. But not because there's gas.

## Reading John Clare on New Year's Eve

If we'd had his Fen eyes, we'd have observed
the mouldiwarp still tunnelling the paved
enclosures: mareblobs, witchens, pinks and pooties
beyond our striplit broadcasts. If we had noted
his words under our engine's hum, the names
that aren't from dead-leaf catalogues of dreams
but rooted in a real place, we'd not be fooled
by furred Celebrity, but know Fame's cold
bleak teeth and face its keeper when he's hanging
his catches on our Auld Lang Syne, singing
of what cannot be changed, not what's on sale.
When we had heard that distant New Year bell,
we would be carrying his black truths by heart
across our thresholds, not thumbing a remote.

# Causeway

Imagine all those dark
timbers revealed
in the damp, dripping
square of Flag Fen:

the sinister causeway
a family tree
that endures beneath
our flat screen lives,

our futile speed-
dating fertility
quest, a huddle
of lost responsibilities.

We look back through
the surface they believed
was the way in
to a better world –

the sacrifices, broken
implements, battlefield
trophies, the lines
of splintered promises,

invisible and unable to
survive once exposed.
Slowly eaten by sugars,
they will dry out

and die under the glare
of children powered by
a new electricity
generated where the

causeway is pointed
that charges their phones,
their games, their pods
as they drop into the darkness.

*To Laurence Binyon*
*(British Museum)*

### I

The screams of the grown-not-old:
they hover on the edge because

there is a centimetre of mud,
because the tunnels are scary,

beechnuts lie unexploded,
a pibroch coils from an old man's

tracksuit bottoms. There is a room
full of double vision and a room

full of mud smell, a stack
of rusty shell cases, a heap

of reeled-in wire. Health
and Safety smile and leave

as a hand from the shelving darkness
reaches for our six euros.

### II

This is one man's dream
of a museum, like

entering a nightmare
behind glass cases –

not because of the ghastliness
of the exhibits

but the manner of the layout:
a fox, stuffed, laughs

in every corner, at
the dummy girl with a hanky

over her nose, the teddy
beside the empty shell-case,

the welcome mat with
'Battle of Passchendaele

1917–1987' on its
grubby grey. Somewhere

Churchill smiles 'Let us
go forward together,'

a nymph is emptying her urn
and Baby Jesus writhes at

the foot of a motorbike.
What is behind the locked door?

'Remember Belgium'

# So it Runs

like the ink
on Magna Carta

like the sewage
outflow at Barking

tides of liberty
tides of oppression

Traitor's Gate
or Thames Gateway

days of Frost Fair
nights of Blitz

the tug that steams
the Fighting Temeraire

into a setting sun
or a rising sun

Händel to Handel
Spenser to Spencer

the hulks in the marshes
the bodies, the toll

of the Bowbelle
and the Marchioness

earthly paradise
earth hath not anything

rain, steam, speed
a lost Maidenhead

so it runs
with no barrier

except the Barrier
and in my memory

a few sandbags

# In Trafalgar Square

Among the forbidden pigeons, they have gathered
as in any other summer: the latest
security threat won't stop them, the weather
has gone on feeding them. They flutter requests

to have their picture taken at the paws
of Landseer's imperial colossi – less often
below that armless, legless, pregnant torso
and head that coos triumphantly at Nelson,

who turns his back on her, inspects his fleet
of lamp-posts down the Mall. Can he see the queues
in Terminal One from there? Some top nob's sights
must be on war, but no one moves, unless

ascending the steps into the National
to catch the *Embarkation of St Ursula*,
check out a *Flight into Egypt*, or a flash
of pale-skinned *Bathers*. Art mocks Life and Terror

is *trompe l'œil*: so, go climb the plinth, adopt
a lion, and play I'm King of the Column,
waving to camera phones, or have yourself snapped
between two yellow-jacketed policemen.

*August 2006*

## *To Siegfried Sassoon*

No need to fantasise a tank
coming down the stalls, it's all
on the hotel TV: dancing girls
flick to Iraq and back
to pop then Palestine
and off again. Music hall
has taken all the tanks
in the world and rolled them out
to keep us dumb and silent
as these, known unto
database and CCTV.

# *Yeats Dances*

## I

Reel with the dog walkers
out along the strand
from Rosses Point.
Lament the absence of the Sidhe.
Note the metal man.
Remember the stolen child.
Jig away from the ice-cream van,
the poop-a-scoop, the rolled back
roofs and muffled radio
until you see it beating beyond
the fields, in its crouched
ascendancy: Ben Bulben.

## II

Weaving in and out
towards the one true
isle, expecting a queue
of rent-a-quote-
and-boat day trippers,
your road disappears

off a jetty. Ironic
applause from the lake.
You're like a pavement
performer so intent
on eyeing the prettiest
smile that you've missed

a simple catch. Balls
tumble and the joke
has spread to the hills.
You have become a stock
Englishman, low
ripplings at your bow.

## III

All that is left
is a stage
and she the last
romantic interest

a chorus girl

who is our daughter
holding her red umbrella

pretending

to be sinking
under the turf
as she treads the raised
foundations

looking cool.

## IV

Steps that are hard
to learn: but follow

the master as he sits
watching the dancer

and the dance, music
passing under his window,

and let your feet
attempt the slippery

winding rhyme and
clause and line

break up to the
battlements where you

can see the whole
country, where you

can see the stars
move in patterns

everyone knows
but no one knows

how to follow,
so hard the steps.


V


Pixels do their digital
flicker and tinkle
in the twilight. Abducted

by memory card, I'm
danced up around
Ben Bulben, cropped

and Photoshopped
to fit the image of
the poet, then

bumped down on to
this wet landing strip
where Mass is just beginning.

Remember your sister
once deliberately danced
on Wordsworth's grave?

You could stage *Lord
of the Dance* in the car park
they've made of Yeats's

and, yes, silver chairs
are out, the golden tea towels
ready in the gift shop

so this old time coachload
can draw breath, while I –
in my green raincoat – cast

the necessary cold eye.

# Dropping Slow
## Lines for Dennis O'Driscoll

I think of you as one of these cranes
rooted in the centre of Dublin –

yellow power grid of trinities,
meccano Book of Kells, lit at night

by a moonglow title on the sky
and a single bright red pulsing star.

You swing above the networking streets,
a grey set of tombstones on your back,

concrete counterbalance that gives you
the light touch, pirouetting to a

wittily apt angle, a deftly
bowed answering theme. Why do they wear

hard hats in your company? Because
you like to wind up big hollow pipes

and drop them back where they ought to be,
then raise with your few taut lines a skip

full of the dark, and carry it off.

# Odyssey

Huge wide screen. *Thus Spake... 2001:*
*A Space Odyssey* – that school trip we made
when I was fourteen, voyage from the sun
out to farthest consciousness, a parade
of life's possibilities that had begun
for me with the Apollo programme and played
*The Blue Danube* and *Atmosphères* throughout
my teenage years. I'd been an astronaut

since watching how my last heroic crew
of single figures burnt up like those nine
birthday candles, too near the sun. I knew
where I must aim: her doppelgänger shine
each morning or each evening, warm and blue
and wrapped in cloud, impenetrably mine.
A Saturn Five would boost me there, away
from childish things, to love's half-year of day.

That mission was aborted. Skies turned red.
We moved back from the light. Our TV screens
began their nightly shower of wounded, dead,
fragments spun where a planet once had been,
destruction circling us. Yet in my head
I dreamed soft landing, peaceful dusty green
from melting ice-caps, lichen, lost canals, dunes
to play in, a comforting pair of moons.

And now I look up from an easy chair
and pick out one gas giant, perhaps two –
a guilty red spot or a halo there.
It all seems so far off. I am not who
I was then at that Cinerama, where
a trinity of beams above me threw
incarnate mysteries of light and space
from a source blinding for a child to face.

## To the Sun (After Akhenaten)

Glorious as the hills in the east now
it spills light, at sea level.

Feast from its prehistoric silver
plate, these dateless riches,

released at last from the tyranny
of sunlessness, of light starvation.

A distant fact, an elephant-in-the-room
dictator, retiring, then flaring

beyond the trace of any probe,
we forget you, plugged into our

electric shadow, drowning in dazzling
gloom, asleep under sodium,

among coiled, low-energy dreams:
we dare not look at one another

unless it's through a screen, strangers
steal our identities, friends become

spot, rash, stroke… feverish,
we forget that you have even set

and are rising already over Al-Hadr,
the swastika lands, the dragon cities,

the thorny paths of Wuriupranili.
But dawn comes, though we ignore its

sacred polyphony, an alarm call
from *Star Trek*, the kettle boiling, cars

as they tick, the radio chatter:
it will be hot, there will be flights

towards your smile, which says *I am here*
*behind ceiling tiles, rafters,*

*insulation, slates and slaty rain-*
*clouds, beyond volcanic ash.*

*Bathe, bask, bare all, ride*
*your chariot, let us be gas guzzlers,*

*my fingers touching that prominence*
*to bless your bones and infiltrate*

*the days, the years.* And do not raise
the subject *x*, the item *gamma*

as we apply the UVF to our children
by the sea, and do not listen to what follows

the pips (the fission, ozone, carbon
dioxide, fusion and confusion).

Let the chick come unmutated
from the egg. Let it come crowing.

Crops must be warm. We must put up
with polytunnels. Keep the cliffs secure,

till desert and its wildfires stagger
over the horizon. Respect the winter,

don't give your smouldering horses
rein such as will hurl us all

to a solar arc. You watched us rise.
Don't let us be washed away

in rolling news. We do not understand
the gravity of your stare, the currents

above or below, we simply know
time and tide, it never rains,

make hay, the switch that says on/
off. We block, we quit the field.

The turbines begin to turn, but you
are the only god we believe in, even here

in East Anglia: as on the West Bank.

*See note on p. 86.*

## To Rupert Brooke

This picture shows you
on a stretcher at Port Said,
no longer the golden boy in
the golden room, no honey,
but heat and a mythology
grown molten. April,
and your blood poisoned.
First of the poets, you were
'a stream flowing entirely
to one end' and the one
we reach for still, your
'The Soldier'. Even Blair,
despite Iraq. We like
the thought of that field
within our power. So there
you lie, about to die
but not until St George's,
when they'll bury you
on Skyros, Achilles' home,
and watch the trickle begin,
(from brook to river to flood)
out of this dry island.

# Wadi Halfa

We never made it to Wadi Halfa

but a dry hot wind from the name
touches me, and floaters begin to drift

nomadically into view on the edge of
travelling dreams, the ones by carriage

and track, or more opaquely in vitreous
humour through mirage and rock – strange

tents from which we come forth by day
with dew on our skin. We did see

Abu Simbel, that film-set for a
captive audience of four, staring

out at Lake Nasser, their heads
full of nothing but Rameses; and heard

the cannoning of one craft against another
as we drifted home, encased in a miniature

funeral boat above the cataracts,
beneath the 'imperishable stars', where 'God

will make it simple'. But Wadi Halfa
would be the thousand and second night

when light drains sacred power
out of Nubia to a dull, mapped

future existence, the final story,
new pylons for old. We were content

with Agatha Christie at the First Cataract
or Kitchener's undrowned island, or over

hibiscus infusions in our flat to spell
that dry possibility of a place called

Wadi Halfa from the bright side
of the English dam. It seemed a point

where mystery must have long been solved,
dissolved, beyond any reconstruction, where

Africa began, our story, and your source.

# Colonial

*(Geoffrey Woodland, 1924–2010)*

A wheelchair and a Zimmer frame,
a stairlift like the scariest ride
in the British Empire Experience

and, upstairs, another wheelchair,
a catheter, a bell perhaps. He did not
put up with such indignities

when he walked out in his white
dress uniform with the Sultan.
In the spare room, a wrinkled

image of Zanzibar. The sword
he wore now feints from the wall
as the ghost train departs.

The topee – only fit for a sketch
or a Merchant Ivory epic –
kept the sun from a head

that had decisions to make, addressing
an unforeseen desire to climb
from the dark hallway to that landing

where Conrad and Kipling hear
Dr Mohammed call, and letters
from America speak of a visit.

### *To Rudyard Kipling*

All the minor keys
have gone underground

to play Butterworth
or Gurney; the smiles

are in these white rows
tinkling ragtime to

the afternoon sun and
in the innocuous whine

of a dentist's drill attending
to one of the fallen.

\*

Twelve thousand voices
in micropolyphony

sing at God's bright
curving wall

which can only echo
thirty-five thousand times

with its own
plaintive: *know this one?*

*this one? this?*

# Africa

*for John Haynes*

Through the whitewash and watering holes of Cowplain,
along the cambers, ruts and rollercoasters of Ryde,
and at the visionary edge of Hatchet Lane

no vuvuzela or lovebird or lion king
but a sanctus broadcast over sand, chalk,
clay, unending rapefields, the low swing

of a bushbaby entering Hunts by night,
Dido's lament at the side of the road to Havant,
a festival of black humour on the Isle of Wight.

*To Julian Grenfell*

Whatever your chances of survival as
a poet, those scenes on Brighton Pier

in *Oh, What a Lovely War!* remain
your legacy. We turn the handle

on the greasy wooden boxes here
in Sanctuary Wood: twin images

try to merge. Not what the butler,
but what the son of the Baron saw.

Your view of Ypres as one 'big picnic'
shapes our view of it as a slaughter.

We have seen munitions laid out
for hungry youngsters. They smell the mud-

caked offerings of how many
thousands who are human jam. 'Dig in!'

you laugh, now the earth is warm with spring
and girls in white are on the downs

and men sing out 'And when they ask us'
as the credits roll. But when we dug

we only found the jawbones and moustaches
of a lost hierarchy, and here a greyhound's

leash, a whip, a padded glove,
some mallets and a stirrup, with sculls

inscribed, in faint blue: Oxford.

# *Hounslow*

## I
heard today
that the roof of my old house
had been ripped off by the vortex created
when the engines of a low-flying airbus made their
final approach

exposing                          my first
bedroom                          and its
steam                             train
wall                              paper
to the invisible night sky        to fly-by-wire and a testing
                     testing
                     howl
                     from
                     dark
                     interiors

# *Heath Row*

A jet tips tail first towards the runway
where the tarmac has started to gleam and steam
and peel itself back revealing hardcore, then gravel,

then loam, then clay, a flint-flicker of glass
passing, flowers into bulbs, beanstalks to shoots,
sails slowing to ungrind wheat from manchet,

to heath that is bog that is scrub that is forest
clearing, clearing so a sarsen can now rise
for this reverse procession of darkening beards

where blood is uncongealed into a newly membered
body, led below deramifying mistletoe
on oak trees that have begun to shrink to nothing

but thunder followed by lightning and an up-pour to the
horizon of ice fronts, advancing, retreating
as the earth shudders, floods, howls, ignites.

# Cycle, with Cytologist

Looking back, we did nothing but laugh at her
green bike, wire basket, three stiff gears and pedal-
powered lamp. Before it was stolen, that 'Shopper'

was her delight and she was the Grand Lady
of the Great West Road, scorning the dragon sleep
of rush-hour. But how to remain steady

at Gillette Corner when you have to keep
glancing round… That's why we gave you a mirror
like the Lady of Shalott, and then a yawping

slughorn fit for Roland. I've a child's horror
of that razor's edge, long for her release
from the dark tower, the curse. Now, *tirra-lirra*,

she comes winging towards us out of the West
Middlesex's bright labs, tracking cervic-
al cancer through a dark glass. Smear. Stain. Test

results, and laughter. The glass she would never
consult, I see now, was one that knows more
about the juggernaut that's coming over

the brow at your back, that's carrying cures
to all disease, that shows Persephone's
route home, past birth and love and all the winters.

# Middlesex

Whatever I've grown into, all took root
in Thames alluvium, old orchard lands,
among the fireweed of the bombsites, slew
of post-war housing schemes. Before main roads
rolled over sarsen stones, their carriageways
advancing west with new light industry
from Firestone to Gillette to IBM;
before the runways and the terminals
for sun worshippers put their capstone on
the last Druid temple, there was Middlesex:
no 'Greater London' then, our tiny borough
the twin heraldic circumstance of Heston
and Isleworth, but Hounslow's where it was.
A suburb, full of cul-de-sacs and semis,
yet trailing clouds of its distinctiveness
among the kerosene-fuelled daylong baying
from Heathrow, keeping in its livery
a memory of its base reputation:
that here began the Heath, here at the Bell,
where gibbets stood for lovers to admire
like dressed shop windows, while travellers drank
or prayed themselves to readiness. Listen.
Now, clear and clean beyond the vapour trails
of pod and sim card, you can still make out
its ringtone echoing.

## To One Who Was With Me

even as we look
at the lists of names
another is added

•

the cross loses power,
feathers, and so
the craft fails

•

it has been whispered
at your ear, no
official telegram

•

a falling bird
a sudden
black dissonance

•

like that voice from
the concrete path
at Tyne Cot

•

a woman calling
the roll
to empty air

## *To Edward Thomas*

Edward, we're going to look for your grave
at Agny (something to do with sacrifice?).
I doubt somehow that we will find it
so off the beaten track.
                                        But that was you,
to take the road less travelled. We wouldn't
expect you to be with the hordes of the dead
at Tyne Cot or on a wall of names.

You died at an observation post.
You looked and looked, and saw the detail
we do not.
                    Today, there is a thick mist.
We head towards Beaurains to find you.

*

And here, beyond allotments, next to back
gardens where a Frenchman mows his lawn,
you are. And there the tall foliage
lours, and, yes, the speculative rooks
are chorusing you. Even – just then –
a woodpecker digging out its round hole
to hide in.   P.E. THOMAS     POET

# Hiraeth

In the kitchen she extemporised laments on a penny whistle,
*Give Me Your Hand* and *When the Tide Comes In*,
as her grandmother leant on the dry-stone wall and cried
to the thistles across the land, to the Church in the Sea.


# Eglwys Llangwyfan

Surrounded at high tide, and still used
for worship during high season, the Church
in the Sea, where we stand congratulating

ourselves on one calm sunrise after Friday's
scourging breakers. These three have spelt
their names in clam and cockle on the rocky steps

that climb up to St Cwyfan's. They have
the old religion, but – to the oystercatchers' orange
warning *hwyl* – I feel the tug of an older

beneath eight centuries, beyond their shells,
that this stony path across the strand
leads west to, where a name in the turf

unnests a long-drowned Londoner.


*Aberffraw, Anglesey*

61

# Home Office

In school uniform, as usual, we look
at solemn marches past the Cenotaph,
then later, at Grandpa's, laugh our heads off
through *Candid Camera*, *Popeye*, *Charlie Drake*.
'And after the Lord Mayor's Show,' says Grandpa,
'the dungcart', turning the gas down, giving me
a go at his pipe, putting on ITV.
No talk about the first or second war –
those racing gun carriages on the Somme,
Dad's Iceland saga (all in Morse), Mum's Blitz –
this minstrel show's enough for them, although it's
American and camp and monochrome.

But take me to the stained-glass-window door,
and up the chessboard-pattern garden path
out of that house, its smell of aftermath
and curing tobacco leaves. Inheritor
of images of Occupation Road,
I've seen the postwar pinstripe regiment
advancing on a Royal Tournament
of jobs and homes and kids. We begged for blood
and bawdy. We got Kenneth Clark in colour,
a boiler, a car. All the piano keys
are swollen, shamed. In its Edwardian case,
the frozen pageantry of that front parlour.

## *To Vera Brittain*

You sit with his uniform
trying to calculate the trajectory
of the bullet

                I see you
only as Shirley Williams or
Cheryl Campbell
on TV

But Roland to the dark tower
came and left this clean
white memo
of sun

            You smelt
the mud and felt
the truth

             that there
was no way out

that you were lodged near
your own heart, with
your own name

# Piano

It belonged to my mother's uncle –
a sailor, who died
at twenty-one
falling from the crow's-nest.
Why had he bought a piano?

*Why did you want me*
*if you didn't know how*
*to play me? If you*
*were going to be away*
*at sea for weeks on end?*

*It was love, even*
*without candelabra*
*and though she was far from*
*grand – a secondhand*
*front parlour upright.*

It stood in a blizzard of glass
when the buzz–bomb
stopped above
my mother and the front door
ended halfway up the stairs.

*The day you climbed*
*the crow's nest in answer*
*to a bosun's pipe*
*were you dreaming of*
*my gap-tooth smile?*

*Her rosewood ribboned*
*with gold, those little*
*brass pedals, a heart*
*felt hammering*
*beneath her lid?*

It has been tuned by Mr Dove
to accompany rock-a-bye-
baby, *The Community Song Book,*
*Mikado, Oklahoma!*
and a hundred Christmas carols.

*And as you climbed*
*did you reach out simply*
*to play what you heard*
*what you desired*
*and so softly fell?*

♪

Its herd of sacred thundering
now feels Mum's
numb fingers
scale the highest octaves
to a dying fall.

# Music Group

*ELGAR*

I'd like to have met you, Edward Elgar.
I'd like to have seen that raw potato
you kept on your desk to clean your pen:

to join in your 'deleerious' laughter when
you play spot the beard or mis-throw
a boomerang, pot red, put phosphorus

in your rain butt. If you've come from *Gerontius*,
don't let me disturb you – just tell me to 'Go
Forth in the Name'. But perhaps one afternoon

in Malvern when you have conjured up a tune
that will knock 'em flat, or found a way to
encrypt yourself inside your *Enigma*…?

*NEW WORLD* (1937)

The Czech Philharmonic
under Szell
cosying up to
London microphones.

A cor anglais plays
plaintively through
the crackle – a fire
that's just beginning
while the players
like servants to the Lord
Chamberlain wait for it
to catch that piece
of paper waving from
the grate, and shiver.

Even the steady pluck
and gut of their Slavonic
strings can do nothing
but follow the beat
until the bar
where the brass will enter.


AMERICAN MUSIC

Samuel Barber asked for croutons to be scattered at his funeral.
From the cortège, as the fresh soil steamed, adagio,
Feldman, Carter, Crumb and all the products of Boulanger
approached to salute and pepper him with their hard pieces.


FIELD

Think of those artists who will never
escape the shadow of one they had
the bad luck to precede, who did

it first but not quite as stunningly
as the name we now remember. John
Field, for example, 'inventor of

the Nocturne', who nodded off while
Chopin opened the five-bar gate
and walked all over him.

# The Mounds at Sutton Hoo

*the burial itself is a poem*
Martin Carver

Walking the perimeter, what is it arcs
over our heads, hurling its song at us?

A lark, nesting behind the barrier, among
the eighteen mounds, beyond the glider trench.

I think of Mrs Pretty hovering here, or perched
in her wicker chair on the edge of events,

who has given all her treasure to the country:
she is a name, a song, a long generous

trilling as we approach the viewing platform.

\*

Where Basil Brown, part sideshow novelty,
part shaman, came prodding his Chaplincy

into a mound and found (to the whirr of a '30s
cine-camera) he could turn old rivets into

a longship – when the gold leaf blew
about in the wind and they gathered pine cones

from Top Hat Wood to make their fires,
production goods in their pockets, rabbits, a dove –

he could take the pipe from his mouth and with a word
conjure from his trilby a head with a crown.

\*

Warrior: his cloth-wrapped pattern-welded sword and helmet.

Host: a nest of silver bowls, the drinking horns, a lyre.

Leader: his boar-studded clasp and stag-tipped sceptre.

Sailor: a maritime repair kit, some tar, an axe-hammer.

Human: with his comb and razor, slippers, games and goose pillow.

*

'They reconstructed me,' says the acid that bites
behind the silver mask in the exhibition room,

'and chased into my surface images of war
you barely reflect on now.' Churchill broadcasts

into Widow Pretty's bedroom where she saw
figures on the mounds and remembers point-

to-point with the Colonel. At the lips
of the burial, bracken is dampening.

She makes an appointment with her medium.

*

| .303 rifles | .88 grenades |
| 2" mortars | Sherman tanks |
| | |
| target practice | as Edith Pretty |
| gasometer heiress | dies   they grind |
| | |
| ignite and sear | trembling fronds |
| above the one | vessel making |
| | |
| its own way | home from Dunkirk |

*

Do you hear the strings of something for harp
that could be Britten? The wind over the ribs,

the rivets like valves into the dark,
the percussion of rain on a tarpaulin, jewels

falling to a note, a chord, and the river
in the distance letting its masts tick in time

to the time that passes, 625 to
1939 to now, and then...

*

Children caddied around the eighteen holes
of their schooldays, checking off facts

they will utterly forget as they try to get
themselves on to the pin of the green.

*

A book sale in the converted mews.

We choose a dozen novels, only to notice
they are all by women. Between the labia

of the slash lay the vanished man. Over the hill
disguised as a biker in a blank-eyed helmet

he screams Mrs Pretty all the way to Ugley.

*

Sand bodies. They can be moulded
in silicon rubber to make fibreglass

replicas for visitors. Enriched with aluminium,
lanthanum, strontium, barium,

insoluble compounds, they leave their mark
even when all clues to this high-ranking

individual have gone, and all his grave
goods are copper sand, iron sand.

*

My dear friend Jürgen – a Sandmann
and an analyst – tell me, as you take

the western ferry out of Germany, why
these people suffered ritual trauma

and were buried here beneath a gallows
while their warlord was honoured in his ship

and why their bones rot but their bodies
survive as sand grotesquery, Pompeiian

sculptures in an hourglass. And why another
Sandmann died of war long after it, time

blowing between us now across East Anglia.

*

These, then, are the eight horizons: from turf
to sand to rabbit hole; through trench to burial;
beyond ploughing to forest floor and subsoil.

And there the small boy sits with his fishing rod
at the edge of a mill pond in Holbrook
at sunrise, whistling *Dr Who*.

*

What are these lights over Rendlesham Forest?
There is talk of UFOs, the Ministry

of Defence has grown defensive and the US
Air Force will only answer calls with the words

'This is not a secure line'. The flash
of a blade, or light on a gold buckle;

the entry of a figure in a cloak, his eyes
dark sockets, his head robotic, minatory,

and words caught on cassette: 'It's definitely
coming... a strange small red light... weird.'

*

Still stuck in the ford at Willy Lott's,
the wain is in no hurry. Rædwald

has come and gone; they have removed his
possessions to London. The demand for hay

is as high as it ever was. The horseman's
whisper goes on colonising the grass at Sutton Hoo

but in the British Museum, Man-Yee Liu
works on a 'bridle block', its animal

contortions, its leather and gilt, the human faces.

*

She lies beside me in a plastic mask
that hisses its milky answer to the riddle

of sleep apnoea; it rattles alliterative
snatches out of Sweet, condenses night

into kenning: my lark-tonguing
serpent swallower, hoard of the bed,

breath's silver droplet dreams,
mounds the green man gallops.

*

A podzol in the country's life, it has been
worked hard, but English Heritage does not want

this double o, an empty name, a myth.

Let rhizomes own it, then, and burrowers
disseminate its history hole by hole.

*

A triple burial.
                    We wave her off
from Saxmundham station, where a guard hands over

a token for the single track and the booking office
is a tunnel to nowhere.
                         A decapitated man
and two women shadowed in the sand.

The holiday ends.
                    Look at this picture.

*

A heath, a new-built country house, where Frank
and Edith Pretty pose on horseback between

the wars, before they have had time to fill
their fifteen bedrooms. There is a law

of Treasure Trove and one that says leave
the dead in peace. But she is forty-seven,

pregnant, and he has left her a regimental
uniform, a sword, a helmet, empty chambers.

The plough runs on. The lovers disappear
behind each mound in turn, and farmers spread

their coprolites and acid as good Mr Fison says
they must, so yields will ripen on the hoo.

A Saxon mast, a plucking string, the plough
runs back, and in the gasp of an eye nine maidens

suckle all the archaeologists of England.

# Waldo Williams in Perry

*O ba le'r ymroliai'r môr goleuni…?*\*

There is a war on and a pacifist
from Wales cannot expect to be enthroned
the way the GIs are when they come down
from their airbase. The master has been housed

between two fields that planners hope to drown
to make a reservoir for English water:
from there he won't escape each dawn departure
of B-17 formations as they drone

eastwards. But he looks west. Perhaps a year
since Linda died – had they been married three?
How few return… that distant, extempore,
low cough. Now all he wants is peace and here

to write his finest work. At *Sunnyside*,
where Bed and Breakfast vacancies recur
as dreams of pass and peak and dripping ferny
ravine, this Mr Williams lived, and did

teach schoolboys Latin conscientiously –
but kept his conscience dry, to make words think
why they were being drilled; nor ever drank
the light that would soon spread from Perry's sleep.

\*'Where did it roll from, the sea of light…?' (Waldo Williams, 'In Two Fields')

# Aldermaston

Hit it, you hit the core
of our nativity, hit
at shadows where the petrol
pump glares NO SMOKING
above the hidden source
of fire and horsepower,
hit brick where a satellite
dish serves the thunder
clouds their light refreshments,
hit this newly wrought
OLD FORGE sign shut
with a clang into a garden
out of *Country Life*...

Hit it, you strike sparks
from the Devil's Punchbowl,
choruses from Grime's
Graves, Wayland's Smithy...
Woden, Thor plunged
red-bodied into our
cold, clean element
hissing their ancient rights
to oversee, to aim
the unsinkable iron prow
and arm you with the earth
strength of a bulging
phone-book full of Smiths.

## *Summer*

### Ernst Stadler

My heart's standing up to its neck in yellow reaping light:
land that is ready to be harvested while the heavens smile.
A scythe-rattling singing will be heard through the fields soon.

My blood, in its marinade of happiness, attends,
absorbed completely by the noon heat.

The barns, the silos of my existence, bare for so long,
will let their entrances swing wide as lock-gates
and over the floors a golden vintage, an inundation, flow.

# *Bugles*

## Georg Trakl

Under the pollarded willows, where sunburnt children play
and leaves are bursting, the bugles call. Churchyard tremors.
Flags in a scarlet stream among the grieving sycamores.
Cavalry through fields of rye, the mills stand silently.

Or shepherds are singing through the night, when a stag
will step into the light of their fire, the ancient ululation
of the grove, dancers raised before a dark partition.
Flags in a scarlet stream, laughter, delirium, the bugles.

*Dunkerque*

## To Charles Sorley

*Wandrers Nachtlied*
sings it: 'England.
I am sick of the sound

of the word.' Wanderer,
your name means,
Sorley. What it sounds

is too quickly mistaken
for something else. You loved
Germany, and died

in France, a Scot.
But you never escaped
your old school, its shades

closed round you even as
truth forecast you
away from Brooke's

'if I should die'
into a weather of
your own making, Sorley's

weather, Graves would
call it, on that autumn
night in Loos

when you found a spook
song – *Süsser Friede* – bursting
from your vanished mouth.

78

## *To Robert Graves*

If each of your years
were in a military grave

with its register and
altar and its portion

of forgetting among
the ninety plots


If your lifetime's work
were so many words in stone

and not the kind of swinging
dummy stuff your pals

Sassoon and Blunden will
bayonet shouting TRUTH


Time would still erode
your corpus, your body

of work, whether poetry
or prose: I, Claudius,

Jason, Juan, or White
Goddess, goodbye to all

That noise like soldiers
tossing stones on to ice

is the rookery. *You should have
died with Sorley*, they cry

to the graves graves graves
graves graves and Graves

# Grodek

## Georg Trakl

The sound of the October woods at evening
is of death machines; golden open fields
and sky-blue waters, the sun patrols
ominously; night puts its arms around
dying infantry, a raw keening
from their shattered mouths.
Yet quietly, among the osier beds,
a red cloud, seat of some malevolent god, gathers:
the lost blood, the moon's chill,
all roads lead to a black dissolution.
Underneath the night and stars' gold hatching
sister's shadow traces through a blank copse
to welcome ghosts of heroes, their bloodied heads;
and among the reeds, grainy flutes of autumn gently play.
Oh, misery the more proud, you bronze altars,
the spirit's hot flame is fed today by a potent agony:
the grandchildren unborn.

# Forge House

*for Valerie, in memory of our mother*
*Betty Greening (née Turner),*
*born May Whale*

He leans out of the door to the forge, holding a smile
that might be simple courtesy or satisfaction
with something he's made, but could be because of knowing

more than us – about the craft of the smithy, of course,
about the anvil itself, even, there next to him
and what its beak and stern are for. But we know nothing

about the secret of our mother's birth, which is here
where he – this smith – once lived, who signed the certificate
that gave her first name to oblivion. She is dead

and didn't know she was born in a forge in Otham
or that her name was beached here on the coast of Kent – rib
I etch into chains of scrimshaw. Her childhood was fixed

to a lathe and she was turned to what we knew. But what
(between one shoe and the next) he knew of the you-shape
crying its luck above him…? Look how his right arm's wrought.

# Kentish

I have stood here before
and still do in a home
movie stored somewhere
up in our bedroom.

Waves approach in lines
from Shakespeare and Keats:
their grey bulks, thins
and sears, then beats

against the harbour –
smearing words
from the greenboard
into chalk novas –

and cappuccinos
the 4.30 cars
and that couple who've seen
a ghost ferry pass

through a channel of mist
where turbine surveillance
keeps turning like lost
reels from old silents.

# Awre

_'where the surname was first noted'_

It is a hopeful name to be born to.
It promises Spring; it sings of pickings
from a lost family orchard, an Eden

on Severn banks, a fruit that is ripe
yet always green. Hold it to your cheek
for the faint enigma. Lick it, your tongue

buds an estuary. Cast, it will bob
the equinox deep into English
etymologies: grig and girn and groin...

Watch it running on a playing field
with others of the inner city, picked on,
nicknamed, yellowed to a cartoon brat.

Or beneath the hundred thousand crosses
left by men who could never spell
themselves, imagine it grinning from their skulls

or groaning in the pelvic bones of women
who bore it, a surge from this serpent bend
of the river into every green corner.

# *Note on Akhenaten's* Hymn to the Sun

Akhenaten may be best known today as the subject of Philip Glass's minimalist opera. But his place in history stems from a decision to shift from worship of the old gods approved by the Theban Priesthood to a strictly monotheistic religion focused on the solar disc or 'Aten'. Despite the many books written on him and his consort, Nefertiti, little of substance is known about this eighteenth-dynasty pharaoh because the Priests of Amen effectively erased the heretic from history. But in the remains of his palace at Amarna, among the extraordinary informal images of pharaonic family life, a *Hymn to the Sun* is several times inscribed. It is the most celebrated piece of Ancient Egyptian literature (Glass uses it in his opera) and has long been attributed to Akhenaten himself. The *Hymn*'s catalogue of praise for the sun's life-giving power has an incantatory quality, reminiscent of the Psalms – particularly Psalm 104. This makes it quite unyielding to read and hard to 'translate' into anything other than a Biblical register. Since leaving Upper Egypt (at least a dynasty ago), I have occasionally tinkered with the *Hymn* and tried to transmute it into something readably modern, something less monophonic. Perhaps it was a spell of unwonted English summer heat that fertilised this strange and sidewinding new version in me, rather as 'your serpent of Egypt is bred now of your mud by the operation of your sun' (Lepidus's drunken suggestion to Antony). 'To the Sun' is very much a Lowell-style 'imitation' in which I have used elements of other translators' versions (I do not read hieroglyphics) to create a solar poem, whose source is Akhenaten, but which casts a few contemporary shadows.